Just a Little Cage of Bone

Collected Poems

by
Bill Cushing

To JoJo

With my respect
and best regards.
From her brother —

Bill

Just a Little Cage of Bone

Collected poems by
Bill Cushing

Just a Little Cage on Bone

By Bill Cushing

First Edition

Author: Bill Cushing
Editor: Paul Gilliland
Formatting: Southern Arizona Press
Cover Artwork: Can Stock Photo/VAC

Published by Southern Arizona Press
Sierra Vista, Arizona 85635
www.SouthernArizonaPress.com

ISBN: 978-1-960038-10-4

Poetry

Introductory Notes

Just a Little Cage of Bone presents the perspective of an old man looking back on life. I derived its title from a Donald Justice poem I've always admired while I want to honor Lawrence Ferlinghetti's power and influence on writing.

The pieces here have been grouped based on peripherally related topics—history, memory, even sports and music.

I need to take the opportunity to say "thank you" to the members of the Beyond Baroque Saturday skype workshop (Alex, Robin, Mess, Michael, Raven, Slattery, Mary, and Lenora) whose input helps polish my writing. Also, thanks to Gabriela Docan, my Romanian online poetry connection by way of the UK; you've been a tremendous friend and colleague.

Contents

Virulent Evolution

Like most atrocities humanity
has seen throughout history, it begins
small, subtle, almost imperceptibly.

Devious whispers of accusations
spread, then grow to screams of protestation,
but those aren't enough to quell anger
or dissipate dissatisfaction.

Sound-sounding slogans become the pebble
that bothers, then irritates, as the slight
that aggravates, grows into a blight
that feeds on its host and produces
more of its kind, only more pernicious.

Thought becomes movement, then a virus,
inevitably destructive, vicious:
a mindless mob, inexorable until
soon enough, voices turn to action:

the thrown brick, the broken window or door,
the setting of fires. Finally, outrage
ushers in fury and hideous death.

The Last Brooklyn Dodger
(January 9, 2021)

Lasorda's at his heavenly *rendezvous*,
his heart giving its final drop of blue.

He became a foul-mouthed savior
and then his team's ambassador.

Still, before Brooklyn was a borough,
the team began by making heroes.

When Jackie broke the racial limit,
the Dodgers forced all sports to pivot.

Then, a Moses drove them to exile
by denying them space, and meanwhile

as Bridegrooms to the Yankees,
O'Malley packed up the team to leave.

Departing Brooklyn with a series ring,
they bid Tommy *addio* with the same thing.

Fighting Gods and Nature Below the Waterline

Forged from Vulcan's anvil,
the pit snipes labor,
deep in the ship's keel,
upon iron machines,
among generators and diesels,
where pitch and heavy roll
throw the crew
against hot metal.

Invaded by thick heated oil
that floods bilges, nostrils flare
in futile protest, and they taste
acrid grease on dry tongues.

They hear every creak and groan
of steel as valves grind,
reduction gears rattle and grunt;
beat back mounting pressure
while the screech of whistling steam
from boilers pierces the enclave
of this clanking and clattering
underworld.

These are not the ones
who take fire; they live in it—
containing furnaces
while generating
enough energy to drive the vessel.
Its spinning shaft,
propels the ship above and pierces
the seat of Poseidon's power.

Chuck Yeager's Prayer

Allow me to die well.
As others worshipped at the altar of fear,
while waiting for the promised apocalypse
and any end times of drought,
I asked no quarter but this: to make my own rules.

Allow me to die stout,
because being shy doesn't help. The first time
I saw a jet fighter, I shot it down; then,
using a broom handle and in pain, I broke
an unbreakable barrier and punched the sky.

Allow me to die acute
knowing the best of us aren't born, that those
who attain greatness make themselves
by experience and with eagerness, and at that moment
of truth, there are either excuses or results.

Allow me to die in peace,
neither speculating what comes next nor regretting
lost youth. I might move back but would never
concede, and the only milestone I missed
was making it to a century.

Creating a Corpse

the body didn't decay from the inside
but from the amassed and mindless
parasites that festered
to kill a nation

they invaded collectively
permeated the soul of a society
and did
what no congress could
until a shroud of suspicion
of "the other"
descended to mask the land
with either fear
or justification
or rationalization

the inner rot came from outside
with a destruction
brought on one by one

like oncogenes
tens became thousands
to destroy the body politic
with infected thoughts justified
by clinging to affirmed beliefs
poisoned by the certitude
of conviction of those
who
held the approved thoughts
who
carried the right signs
who

wore the appropriate hat
or the most fitting outfit

subversion doesn't need spies
just a marauding cult of zealots
taking action
like the innumerable insects
that can fell an elephant
with a parade of slight
but poisonous bites

First published in *Sixfold.*

Punters at the Track

Dressed in silks, the four horsemen
approach the stalls,
jogging to their call
in steady gait
to wait
for the crack of a starter's pistol.

Then the maelstrom:
Frenzied heartbeats,
quickening blood
pulses in necks
outstretched as frontrunners
spray the field
with clods of dirt
and streaking mud as they
round each turn,
digging in, running the furlongs.

In the stands,
bettors clench paper dreams,
scatter cigar ashes
from pumping fists,
touting
their wagers,
playing long odds,
trying to even
things up.

The field finishes
in equine sweat,
lunging through
the chute, to affirm
who's better
on the bit.

First published in *Feisty Runts.*

Gates of Hell

Prima sezione
The Poet sits atop the lintel
contemplating original sin
while Ugolino devours his sons
and bodies crawl over bodies, grinding
in anguished copulation of need
never satisfied. Surrendering
hope, desperate to attain relief,
they try but know they can never flee.

Seconda sezione
How does one incarcerate Satan
when he was delivered already,
consigned and impaled to sheer stone walls
steep in the depths of searing torture
and guarded with the care of envy?

Terza sezione
Incensed by the erosion of time
that softens and sabotages, the Devil calls
for cacophony between the quiet
lightning revealing feral fortune
as the beauty of desolation
descends into vengeance to fracture
the force of the oppressive thunder
from millennia of violence.
Jealousy transforms rapture into
innate bitterness while the devil,
a species apart, stained by hostile mirth,
poisons and torments those from earth.

Quarta sezione
Because truth can be so easily
misplaced—like extinguishing a teardrop
of flame on a candle between a thumb
and forefinger, one never dares to lie
when confronting the Grand Deceiver.

First published in *The Poet* (UK).

Crashing the Apostle's Cocktail Party

Peter, as always, wants to order first
even though he'll deny that again
and again and again. James reminds him,
"I was the first to join, the first to die,"
which starts the first clash.

"How does a bush burn but refuse to turn to ash?"
Paul bores the Virgin. She twirls a feather that
Gabriel must've left after his visit.
Paul persists, "The only possibility
is the ground's sanctified, holy."
While Thomas seems to have his doubts,
he leaves to go and argue with everyone else.

The most important invitee
is late, but Philip explains in humility
that he seems to be caught
between a rock and a hard place.

While Simon's on the guest list,
not much about him comes to mind
among the other ten
when looking at his face.

Then
things get tense when, shaking a fist,
John the Baptist crashes the affair
and loses his head in anger
over Andrew's desertion while Matthew persists
in taxing everyone's patience.
John, animated as ever,
rails against the rot of such heresy.

Jesus appears just before the bar empties out,
grabs himself a Rolling Rock—
"Second one this week," he claims between quaffs.
Nathaniel, ever the true believer—lackey actually, laughs
at all of his jokes, then notes that Judas
has judiciously turned down the invitation
although he did send flowers, but
perhaps 30 pieces of silver
thistle stems were not the best choice.

Little Boots

Named as a wellspring to honor my godhead.
Still, I got shod and bridled
with that childish appellation instead
of my proper imperial title.
With jewels sewn into my slippers, embedded
into the gunwales of my prams,

I used a gentle voice and a winning smile,
a crocodile lurking under still waters,
attacking rivals, painting my domain,
making it a blood-spattered canvas
I spent three years on the throne
enthralled by violent fascination

until thirty of my protectors, anxious,
employed assassination, impaling me.
They sliced my corpse, scattered the debris
of my ribboned remains onto the palace floor,
then installed my weak-chinned, lame,
and stuttering Uncle Claudius as *imperator*.

First published in *Glomag.*

A Petty Memory: A Part Time Cento

The ground broke open to restless sleep,
silent screams. He stood on stage, eight days
from death, on a night clouded with dreams.
The Hollywood Bowl, packed with all kinds,
all ages, and all down the street.
They stood in line to hear him play,
a self-made man who did it on his own
and could see those fault lines.

They went wild when the lights went down
and twilight made the smog into rainbows
while Los Angeles chariots swung low
and the town lit up, the world got still.
There's something lucky about this place.
Somewhere in some far-off space,
like a cat creeping through the grass,
I will recognize your face.

Hearing his final gig under this dome,
like something from a dream, he was going
home. Thank God for California a place
where you can believe what you want to believe.
After all, it's a great big world
with lots of places to run to, but
Tom gave us the best of everything,
and that was more than good enough.

First published in *Spectrum.*

Kareem

It took forty years of aging to get
you to leave the court, yet
rather than older, you are taller,

towering over everyone
before and, probably, everyone
who will ever come to play.

I was just learning the game
when I first heard the name
Lew Alcindor:

one of only three
who could leap and reach
over the top of the boards

to touch the back. The other two
were Russell and Wilt, and you
were still in school.

You kept the strength of the big man inside—
blocking shots, driving powerful
and smooth as a Coltrane solo.

Then you changed your name
after you changed the game
forever—

from lay-ups to untippable skyhooks:
shots leaving the wrist
from outside the key in an arc

so graceful and perfect they surpassed
pyramids, lunar landings, maybe
even resurrections.

First published in *Aethlon: The Journal of Sport Literature.*

Tower of Pride

... with apologies to Barbara Tuchman,
author of The Proud Tower from which this began ...

Nicholas—well-bred, well-trained,
a failure—married for love,
bringing dreaded Germany
to Russia's throne only to attack
the nation of Bismarck.

Nicholas sired a doomed heir
menaced by the slightest bruise
that might refuse to heal,
a youth whose savior was
a drunk Siberian peasant-monk.

Nicholas felt obliged to save face
by leading a life of bad choices,
causing strife with his subjects,
people he so cherished
that he refused to hear their voices.

Nicholas destroyed Romanov rule
and died known as the czar
who, rather than ascending
any heights, perished,
leaving the family name disgraced.

Sonnet to Slaughter
(inspired by the diary of Robert H. Carter,
private: 22nd Massachusetts infantry)

The ground held no value, the town little use,
except for foot-rotted, grey-clad men
hoping to find much-needed shoes.
What followed was beyond their ken
When groves of peach trees and fields of wheat
Became hallowed witness to brutalities
as lice-ridden troops, bound for defeat,
charged over meadows and fallen bodies.
The banshee wail of the rebel yell
arose with bayonets and shot lead;
cannonade shook buildings, roof tiles fell,
and after three days, desperation led
Gettysburg, then a place of little worth—
now one of lost causes, "a perfect hell on earth."

First published in *Roll Call*. Third place winner in the 2019 Helen Shaible Annual Sonnet Competition.

The Between Days
(written on the 23rd day of the 2020 lockdown)

We now spend all our days
surrounded by wonders
of this age, trapped between
new lines of safety, drawn
farther out, to become
margins of solitude,
forcing isolation.
This pox is not our sin;
rather, this other life
relies upon our lives.
This virus is trying
to live between us, like
all of God's creations.

First published in *2020, An Anthology of Poetry with Drawings.*

Tenor in the Pipeline

Wearing a ball cap, fleece jacket,
and cuffed jeans, the man
with a pony-tail hunches
at one end of a galvanized tube
topped by a half-drunk bottle of beer.

Tapping a dirty work boot,
he plays his tenor sax. The tune
moves through a mile of iron
that stretches along a furrow
that fades into the distance,

a dry moat scooped out
for this pipe resting on
wooden beams where a bike,
propped against them,
waits. Soon enough, this musical

tunnel will be put to use,
but for now, having dug
the man's music, it returns a refrain
while hidden hands
clap a percussive beat.

First published in *Stories and Poems in the Song of Life.*

Bill Cushing*

Playing Ball in the Hereafter

As children, Henry Aaron and Don Sutton
grew up in towns three hours apart
and learned the game between fields of cotton;

then the hitter moved east, the pitcher, west
as they took paths to opposite coasts.
Two All-Stars, they became among the best.

Upon dying, Sutton arrived first and may
have used the time to loosen his arm
while warming up on the clay

waiting for Hammering Hank's arrival.
As they play, now in eternal prime,
celestial fans admire erstwhile rivals

and wonder, from where they sit,
what is the most wonderous display:
the sweet pitch or power-driven hit?

First published in *Sixfold.*

Haka
(written March 2022 to honor Ukraine)

Defeat birthed these primal tribesmen;
harsh turmoil raised them, so they began
celebrating life with clenched fists that
hammer chests, then open to slap forearms.
Blue scars from youth form patterns;
swirls and spirals grow from spacious faces enlarged
by eyes that bulge, by cheeks that widen,
by tongues that snake over jutting jaws.

The air shimmers from muscular vibrations.
They leap and stamp side to side,
slap the ground in defiant rage, a sharp
dance that displays fury for at least
one more day. The warriors offer unbroken stares,
challenge anyone who dares engage:
"Take my head. Gnaw on my bones, suck the marrow,
but never doubt what ferocity we'll return to you."

First published in *The Poet* (UK).

Feeling Judas

It's for the best, I recited to myself
as I drove the woman I took care of,
but never cared for, to her new home.
Once she comprehended the deception,
knew our true destination, she begged me
to turn back, even offering me
her checkbook. It was perhaps the only
moment of pity I ever had for her.
Now I peer into pleading eyes and grip
my son's arm—struggling against his wishes
and the yards of tape bound to keep him
from ripping out the needle meant to nourish.
Meanwhile doctors, nurses, technicians
wrap bandages over electrodes to monitor
the questionable actions in his brain.
A bayonet of betrayal pierces me,
and again, I think: *It's for the best.*

Medicine of Moths

The room even felt dark on
the evening my sister said a
last goodbye to her husband.

Opening my eyes, I pray
for the medicine of moths
to heal her pain

and wrap her like the wings
they fold to envelope
around themselves.

Being caregivers, these shamans
attend to what is heard
instead of seen. They seek

the light within darkness,
using clear vision, trusting
the impulses that begin

upon conception. The moths
create a base that manifests itself
to transform her pain

much as these venerated
totems, now trapped beneath
glass, change themselves.

Bill Cushing

Approaching Auschwitz

A young American approaches,
victorious in the Spring of life,
enters ferrous gates crowned
with razor wire emblazoned
by words wrought of iron
that seem to dance: *Arbeit macht frei.*

Bony arms reach beyond fences
that, for years, surrounded
this place of barely-
living victims. Suddenly,
he feels old, as ancient
as this Polish winter.

Buried beneath snow, he sees
what seem like logs
thrown on the ground. Perhaps these
are packs of sleeping dogs,
but the closer the corporal gets,
the better defined they become

until he bears witness to piles of people:
mothers, children, old men—
all scarred with skeletal smiles—
bodies interred under a row
of tall chimneys that had sent
ash, soot, and what seems like

burnt paper floating lightly
as this snow, freshly fallen
on ground smudged with trails
of boot prints in the cinders—
all that remains of the
friends, family, or neighbors
to those still barely alive,
those shuffling few who survive.
Beneath those cylinders of brick,
squat warehouses keep the debris
of bodies, the burnt skin
seared from bones leaving only a skeleton.

He finds a solitary German
crouched inside one vacant oven,
and in white-hot ire
shoulders his Springfield to fire
round upon round
into the pleading enemy.

The young soldier will leave,
return home to marry
his high school sweetheart,
and raise a family. Meanwhile
never again will he feel
Spring's warmth without tasting bile.

First published in *24ᵗʰ Annual Yom HoShoal* (Holocaust Remembrance)

Foregoing the Franchises

It's difficult to visit Burger King
when memory can recall
the Loop's Chicago Burger,
thick as a thumb
and smothered under Swiss,
or a teriyaki burger and potato salad
chased with a Watney's
at Barney's Pub.

Don't ask me to eat soggy eggplant
drowned in tomato sauce
at Olive Garden
when the firmest is
at El Morfi, a place
where paintings of gauchos
and photos of Buenos Aires
populate brick walls.

I won't be bothered
by Domino's when
there is Domenico's,
filled with the aroma of tiger shrimp
mixed with Alfredo.
Any siren song of Weinerschnitzel
pales to the call of the wild from
Vicious Dogs.

Pardon me, Denny's, but
I cannot resist
the collapsing red neon star
over the Astro diner; it draws me,
like gravity, to a place

where regulars gather,
parking beside black-and-whites
going 10-7 for meatloaf and joe.

First published in *Spectrum.*

Bill Cushing

A Brief Eulogy for an Atheist

"Death is a part of life," say the living, yet
many people will bear burdens to get
one extra day – one reason to admire my father,
a man whose creed rejected even the notion
of an afterlife, then turned down
a chance to go on since it meant
he'd have to exist unable to engage
with the company of people.

First Work

At ten I sought my first paycheck from Mister Kuntsler,
the old man across the street wheezing on a porch stoop,
laid low by emphysema. I'd hear his body struggle, trying
to sing songs he'd sung when young – now chained to heavy tanks
to inflate his lungs. Each Saturday he'd sit behind
a rolltop desk, retrieve his ledger to sign the check
I earned dragging their two metal trash cans
to the curb, three times a week. When needed,
I cut the grass, shoveled snow from the walk.

His signature's scrawled and jagged—the only flourish
he had left in him, but a half-century before,
he'd been a warrior, a Basque who'd fought Franco,
an armed Fury riding horseback through the forests
or across mountains that spanned the Spanish border.
On days he wasn't hindered by breathlessness,
he'd recall those years—invading the plains, then
sleeping on stone beds or hiding, huddled around
clandestine fires set after scaling those coastal steppes.

Once he croaked the words, *Askatasuna eta herrialda*:
"Freedom and country." And in that moment, his face brightened,
his back straightened, and he seemed to shed age.
Often, my jobs done, his wife of 60 years sat with me
at their kitchen table. She poured homemade lemonade,
fed me slices of burnt cheesecake. "From our country,"
she'd say, her aged eyes fixed on her own distant memory.
After he died, she tripled my pay to thank me
for returning her husband a measure of pride.

An Elephant in Iceland

Wrinkled layers of water-cooled basalt,
which for six months erupted as lava
to pour from *Helgafell*, the Hill of Fire,
slumbering on an island that sits and
splits itself between the tectonic plates
of Eurasia and the Americas.

Does the beast that created new land
from crushed buildings and ash sleep as it
faces seaward, or is it drinking the waters
swirling off the shore, eddying along
the "Home Island?" Perhaps this igneous
pachyderm intends to swim to sea.

Las Croabas

Plank by plank,
the snowy egret
approaches, stalking
a crushed milk carton

as a sliver of moon
drops, waiting
between the fading light
of today and the dropping

of night's velvet
curtain that reveals
an array of stars
uncensored by the glow

of shopping centers.
A chorus of coquis,
playing percussion,
ushers in morning.

First published in *Celestial Musings.*

At Pete's Hut One Saturday Night

Cue balls scatter,
clicking through the Marlboro haze
thick enough
to choke a horse.
He wheels around, bearlike hand
gripping the edge
of fading felt.
He stops, says,
"Let's put that puppy right there."
Then, aiming from
an otherwise
awkward angle,
slaps a clean cross-table shot into
the side pocket.

Three girls, sitting
on a bench, watch
as the winning continues.
He is handsome:
broad shoulders, a square
face, framed by
a dark beard, breaking into wide smiles.
And were it not
for the broken
lower half
of his body,
he might have left the place that night
and gone home
with any one of them—
or all three.

First published in *Blue Nib* as "At Pete's Hut".

Witnessing the Fourth in 20/20

Sitting in a steel box that rolled onto a field
joined by other people, they also isolated.

I contemplate the potential to regain
the freedom we did freely yield.

Beyond the wooden skirt draped
before waves of mounded dirt that

wash ashore before a large screen
of flickering images,

we watch as bright strings of confetti
spray across the sky, coming

from illegal fireworks. They burst
and surround a honeyed lunar orb

trapped between power lines and balanced
above peaks of low-pitched parapets.

Surviving "Adagio for Strings"

First
and <u>only</u> rule:

Never listen in the dark or
while vulnerable
for

every heartbreak,
every 3 a.m. drunken phone call,
every failed relationship
      that's been boxed up,
      put on a shelf

will bore its way
out
of your memory
and pierce
your tear ducts

especially
when
enduring
that final,
single, seemingly never-ending and eternal

note.

Marathon

With thanks to Brian, for running me home.

1 - 15 miles
The first stop is to answer nature.
Even after thirteen miles
I am still on schedule,
but two miles later, hunger
becomes a hole widening out
in spirals of distraction
while the cold, wind, and rain become
a team disrupting my stride. Stride?
What stride? Every single joint
from the waist down locks up
in frozen argument; the soles of my feet
are bloody well still there though.

16 miles
A friend's father passes
in an ambulance—for me.
"Need any help?" he asks.
"No thanks. I'm beyond that now."

18 miles
Just the wall is left.
I pass it in detached stupor, thinking,
"So this is what morphine is like."
A mental clearing occurs. Now
nothing will stop me from crossing
the finish. Nothing will stop me
from the pain that is my own.

22 miles
What would Pheidippides think?
He'd laugh, probably,
then say something like,
"We have nothing to fear but death itself."
And that was exactly
what he got.

Finish
Shoes slogging through mud,
I hear my name.
One-quarter mile left
and still standing—
almost running.

First published in *Aethlon: The Journal of Sport Literature.*

Looking for the '20s I Wanted

Let's dance into our next decade
like it's the last century.

We seek Cole Porter naughty
and Gatsby glitterati.

Take the appletinis;
we're going back to whiskey,

straight up, no chaser, leaving low
hip-hop for sly innuendo.

Shun the charm of some Romeo
to dance cheek to cheek

with a new Valentino.
Put the guys back in spats,

with pencil thin moustaches,
who can woo vamps who coo

with throaty voices
promising sexy choices.

Silhouettes of *femmes fatale*
are back *en vogue*. While smoke smolders,

drifting off cigarette holders,
they swing Charleston,

and papa goes Dada as
Samba beats throb on drums

that pound Tommy-gun rhythms.
Trumpets blare brassy tones

alongside the lament of clarinets,
the doppler slide of trombones.

We seek evenings of nightclubs,
art deco cabarets, or passing

some speakeasy's bolted doorway,
finally opened by sentries

after whispering the password:
"We was sent by the twenties."

First published in *Glomag* as "Waiting for the Twenties"

Bill Cushing

Marking Territory:
Federal Building, Westwood

Sprouting out of the ground,
this modern monolith with tinted windows
lets the State look out but prevents
citizens from peering in:
always the ruling classes' preference.

Yea, though I walk through the valley
of high rises, I avoid the anthropophagy
of my age, for the erosion of time
destroys and smooths while people carve
family crests into wooden doors

like businesses with the impudence
to place their logo in the lintel
or set their name in mosaic tiles
at a building's entrance as if they
will forever remain in this place

when eternity rests in men surrounding
tables in the shade. They pass their days
moving dominoes, each one the same
in his tendency to being worthy of life
by not clinging to illusions of eternity.

First published in *Spectrum.*

50

Allison Attempts Suicide

Perhaps she tired of the epilepsy
crowning her life.
Perhaps her socially awkward manner
proved too crippling.

Our lives were separated
by 15 years, but she was
old enough for anguish,
yet too young to see
other options.

How easy,
sometimes, to forget
life's most difficult choices
become the most important.

The choice is ours.
Life may be boring,
terrifying, or trite,
but, above all, one
must stay alive.

Hardest job on earth.

Summoning the Pages

I love pulp I can see, feel;
pages to taste, chew and digest;
versuri made more real

by the musk of their smell
released in understated swells
as they age.

I dive head first into leaves
surrounding and filling me
with joy, sadness, information,

recording the souls of each generation.
They shelter me like protective eaves,
each waiting to provide.

Words become beatitudes
of discovery; others confide
melancholy meditation.

I still refuse to submit
to the new allure of reading a screen
designed by the demon Kindle,

preferring to listen to the crinkle
of paper as it flips,
falling flat against its ancestors.

Even cheap escapism
or the worst of creations
fulfill a purpose,

have a message to tell.
In the end, the pages I've viewed
have all served me well.

Feeding Ritual

To help him cling to life,
she postpones her own.

A tube grows from his side,
a sapling's trunk

that pumps pulpy food into him.
She serves this sacrament

twice-daily, then washes
away her tears as she

washes out the hose that
allows her father to breathe.

Remembering George from House Cat to Alley Cat and Back

The girl next door didn't care that
the kitten she chose "was a girl cat"
when she chose the name
George, yet the moniker matched:
black-on-white fur forming a jacket,
sunglasses, even a "soul patch"—
a real beatnik look. Then George
adopted my family, living the bulk of her life
in our house, returning, periodically
to check in on the O'Hagans.

Two decades later, working
graveyard shift, I came across
Doppleganger George
deep in the bowels of a retirement home:
that same black-on-white beard, but
this time a bit more reticent, needing
more time before true comfort
and contact was allowed, before resting
in my lap while we both napped
before the day shift arrived.

First published in *Paw Prints in Verse.*

GOAT of the Booth

Who'd've bet on this: That on the Second of August
in the Monkeypox year, instead of young Juan Soto,
the rising star wearing the mantle of Mickey,
we'd end the day focused on a 94-year-old
who always looked at home in a suit and tie
by the name of Scully? Vin made sports poetry;
his voice, a singularity of euphonic tones; his iconic prose
turned handheld Made-in-Japan radios into conduits
of prolific knowledge. He was able to share stories
that made men mythic—from Hammerin' Hank Aaron
breaking the Babe's record, his 715th hit to left, out of the park,
even football's "Catch" from "Joe Cool" to Dwight Clark,
and he did it with wit, the way Shakespeare viewed it.
Now the Dodgers embark on the next stage of place;
they've lost their last connection to Brooklyn.
Everywhere, fans wept, feeling no disgrace.

First published in *Spectrum.*

Catalogue

In recent days, I have been wondering
where to place all my previous loves:
do those who taught me to savor life

belong with stalkers who left notes
in strange places? Where do I tabulate
those who betrayed me? I feel obliged

to include those I betrayed, but how
do I classify those who, upon our meeting,
neglected or rejected me?

Life Cycle of
*Alba Mascula, Normalum**

What the Sphinx left out.
A boy is born in a nursery:
hairless, naked, wearing diapers.
As he grows, he spends time
collecting stamps and playing
with train sets until the time arrives
that he develops an interest
in girls, so the chase begins.
Eventually he finds the "one"
and settles down to wedded bliss,
but soon it seems like settling.
His eyes wander; he chases other girls
until finally virility
languishes and energy dissipates
into a time for an old man
to collect stamps and play with train sets.
He ends life in a nursery:
hairless, naked, wearing diapers.

*Straight white male

Reality's Riddle

A teenager's family gathers
to celebrate his birth,
not knowing the next day
they'll prepare his grandmother
for her return to earth.

On an innocuous New Year's Eve,
a doctor observes the passing year
at a party, unaware
she will ring in the next annum
calling her son's hour of passing.

Which is the crueler taking
mortality has in store:
Preparation and foreknowledge,
or blinding ignorance shaking
confidence to the core?

I Want to be Rick Blaine

First, there's the cigarette
sitting in an ashtray by a chessboard.
Smoke curls around the white bishop
that he taps, just once, with a forefinger
before retrieving it.
His other hand rests by a
coupe of champagne.

The strained face peers
up from the white dinner jacket,
weary and pained, an isolated man
with plans within plans. Even when
heartbroken, Rick Blaine appears
the disillusioned mercenary, living
without questions.

More than *noir*, he was forced
into heroic greatness, becoming
the "Hemingwayan hero"
wearing a fedora, its brim angled,
shoulders slouching, nonchalant,
but beneath his body waits in a panther's
crouch of readiness.

Cary Grant exuded elegance;
Newman and McQueen epitomized cool
while Brando rebelled, and Dean
laments and broods,
but Bogart evoked the essence
of all of them to teach me how
to be a man.

First published in *Spectrum.*

The Answer

It's a parade
of animosity and rage,
this age-old melee
between youth
and old age.

Elders view the young
and complain
while youth regards
those graying
with disdain.

The source that's led
to such invective
is an easy shoal
to thread;
it's in the perspective.

Young people see
in the elderly
what they will be,
presenting
one frightening eventuality.

Meanwhile the old heed
what to them is the
idiocy of youth,
and they plead,
"Was that really once me?"

There actually is
no need to guess;
the answer
to both views
is "Yes."

First published in *The Poet* (UK).

Bill Cushing

Under Construction

They work as a team.
Some shovel dirt,
clearing the way;
others follow
leveling earth,
grading the new path
with blades,
laying down
a road that becomes
an artery.

Buildings go up—
the tall ones for offices,
hotels, apartments—
a few
houses.
Intent,
the workers continue,
stopping only
when mothers mount
front stoops,
calling out

"Suppertime!"

First published in *Local News*.

Merchant of Memories
(for Gene)

You left the cold of Rockford, a widower
with a son, to chuck it all and move South.
Opening a market, you sold canned goods,
rooted for the Cubs on a nine-inch screen.

You created a cracker-barrel store with cable,
a gathering place for neighbors, the mailman,
and the janitors from the grade school
across the street. You'll be among the first

I think of when asked about this place, built like
Legos, resting beside a northbound river.
I'll recall the games, beers, smokes, and laughs shared,
and the only wake I went to that decade.

Shoulders squared, short and squat, with bulldog looks:
perhaps you came back as Shorty, the dog who marches,
as you used to—unashamedly,
unabashed—on similarly squat legs.

First published in *Spectrum.*

Observations of Four Modern Women

Sheila
Riding a bus, her lean body draped
on a loose frame, her female figure wrapped
in work clothes, feet dappled by a thin
dusting of cement on steel-toed boots
after her day, operating a backhoe.
Her hair hides under a red paisley bandana
but for one stray corn row.
Another rider detects
the patina of her day's work
in the sweat coating her skin;
his nostrils flare, hoping to hold her,
this child of Ghana.

Kar'in
Hair standing at outlandish angles,
she tries to achieve the statuesque,
and that is precisely what she portrays:
a beautiful, painted, and polished
porcelain figure that—
at the slightest movement, smile, or grimace—
would break and crack, demolished
into shards of broken perfection,
to lay on the ground.

Mejgan
Black hair curls, flowing over
a moon-shaped ivory face
smooth as marble.
A paragon of Afghani beauty,
she is untouchable by virtue
of cultural *rigueur.*

Melody
She dances smiling, hair
bobbing on a head seemingly unattached,
as if spring-mounted to her body.
At the end, her applause is too long,
her shrieks, too bawdy,
too loud, too alone.

Challenging Bumper Stickers

Question authority white letters proclaim,
a battle cry set on a black backdrop,
but should we not do the same?
Let's respond to bumper stickers, challenge
phrases plastered on car rear ends,
simplistic slogans that ought
to stop pretending to be thought,
these rigid deflections
posing as reflections.

Meat is murder, but plants breed,
grow, move, feel pain, bleed, are even aerobic,
so aren't vegans kingdomistic, vegephobic?
Still, that response takes too long. To do it right,
retorts should be short and slight.

Eden was vegan declares another.
We saw how that turned out.
Support our troops, declares an *Army mother*.
As a taxpayer, do I do anything other?
I may be slow, but I'm ahead of you.
Where is a battering ram when one's due?

In case of Rapture, car will be unoccupied:
Rather smug, almost snide.
Doesn't God get to decide?
War is not the answer." Doesn't that depend
on the question?
Every mother is a working mother one says,
but let's recall Gabriel Fernandez.
 Coexist plastered next to the command *Resist:*
No question needed at the irony in this.

Drum Circles Damned by Modern Puritans

Standing askew with a sterling nose ring
that glints from the California sun,
the slouching hipster brings proper 'tude

to the 2022 Whole Earth Fest.
Lobes loop around grommets, sagging
in defiance; baggy shorts barely cover BVDs.

He comes upon a drum circle—men
as pale as himself, copying primal life—
and in nasal tenor commands, "Stop this,

this cultural appropriation."
With that demand, the piercings and ink,
all these trappings cannot counteract

that stench he carries of a junior high
hall monitor who announces himself
and demands respect while clutching a clipboard.

Mary, Colin, and Me

The moon hangs suspended
balanced between three stars
this autumnal February evening.

He's Libra, balanced; you, I,
Pisces—water signs:
tonight a lunar Trinity.

And I'm thinking of him
and you, and his eyes—
your eyes when you allow,

And I think how when
I hold him, I hold a part
of you, and sometimes

that's cnough.

First published in *Poetry Nook.*

Fever Dream

Your grandfather's cult
didn't work; few ever do.

If I cannot earn trust,
allow me at least to achieve lust.

In my nightmare walks
down Vicodin Street,

I endure benadryl visions
where racial supremacysts

kiss Roobha, who dances,
balanced between two worlds.

Forget Big Brother; Big Data
threatens more of us today

Thirty: The Best Year

When I was 45, a 15-year-old announced,
with authority, that I envied his youth.
I laughed.
"Double it, and then you're there."
My favorite year remains 1982, at age 30:
single, obliged to little and making good money
working 12-hour days, six days a week
revamping an Italian tanker in the Bethlehem Steel
Yards, ripping out its fire-scorched innards
to rebuild it into an Apex ship.
On Fridays, we'd visit the Lexington
open air market for bushels of oysters
and cases of St. Pauli Girl or go
to Gunneys to sit and crack steamed crabs.
On Sundays, I'd hit an arcade that sat
between Johns Hopkins Medical Center
and the shipyard where I worked,
diving into its cacophony of sound and light,
an almost perfect midpoint of high tech
with blue collar, I spent hours playing Zaxxon,
saving the universe as I steered my warrior's
craft around obstacles of radiation mines
or between the barbed wire of laser beams.

Evenings I bounced from one
Baltimore club to another, playing
in a single man's paradise, a place where
I sat on the cusp of both Hammerjacks,
even eating the worm in the old one,
while dating women that shipyard workers,
such as I, shouldn't expect to even get a chance
to talk to. So, keep your stage five puberty;
give me thirty.

First published in *Spectrum.*

Siren of Agony
(after *Biohacker-10* by Jenn Zed)

She gags on the cascading gush of blood
she vomited. As it flows down, coating
her chin, she raises two fingers, pressing
blood-stained hands against pale breasts
as life ebbs from one posed in futile supplication.

Trying but failing to stanch the viscous,
acrid cascade of her life force flowing
from within her, she stares toward the sky.
A biohack victim, her vacant eyes
beg, hoping to hear any answer why.

First published in *Glomag*.

Three from 70

Each day's aches become more real, announcing
themselves with ever-pronounced authority
while ease of movement slows under
the crushing heel of the element of
surprise—we greet age, the artist
painting with pain. Time erodes
youth into an ever-wilting
sarcode, a polaroid that
fades, just as it makes
a dragon from a fly,
but unlike that
creature's
lives of
duality,
we are
never
given
more
tries.

Grandfather: Lemuel Gurney

Born, maybe in 1889; likely '88;
don't bother with the day or month.
Passing before I turned three,
I can't conjure his face, but my shoulders
recall calloused hands that cradled me,
his palms infused by the smell of earth.

My mother descended from English courtiers,
but her father hailed from Maine, where
he grew as hard as its granite cliffs,
logging in the White Mountains. Then he moved
to Vermont to build his home in Searsburg,
across from Camel's Hump, high in the Green Mountains

that looked down on Bennington. He constructed a cabin
with tools he made. I knew my grandfather's brother.
He taught me about long guns, showing me
to cradle the wooden stock in the small of my shoulder.
"Breathe steady. Hold it. Exhale slow when ready.
Squeeze, don't pull." My great uncle spoke of his brother,

a man whose life blended into nature,
a man hunting squirrels when doctors
ordered him to bed rest after surgery,
a man who slathered his arm with maple sap
to attract bees and prove a point: "See?"
he'd growl. "They don't attack, only defend."

Lighting Shadowed Designs

While singularly high on chem-trail theories,
a mad Ulysses whose image might hide past
icons for a lucid siren. Then he saw himself
in others, survived by living more obscure
and even stranger lives. Elements of surprise
invited a state of being, frighteningly
similar and rivaling unself-conscious
recycling, twisting reality slightly
when the muse struck hard and fast and repeatedly
with a club. Images, like party crashers,
with faces that clash with nature, fractured color,
shade, or hue. Lives are altered forever
through brute evolution of thought, and living, like
finding Nessie—ever sought yet rarely seen,
dissolves into a series of hallucinations.

First published in *Otherwise Engaged.*

Prime Question

We drink
while all around us,
people,
including ourselves,

die.

Beer helps,
but
not enough.

It's easier to ignore
unanswerable questions
than to ask,

and then face
the consequences
for asking.

A Prayer to Reject Sanctuary

Let me live
alive,
unnumbed by the sedative of
too much comfort,
too much security.

Let the pain of age and isolation
sharpen my senses,
hone my soul
into a spear tip of exploration,
excommunicated from
the swaddling of outside help.

Keeping children safe
presents its own danger.
I was battered and bent,
dented in a thousand ways;
past damage altered me.
Every scrape and scar, each cut or burn,
ordained me into the one I became.

The Prodigal Father

Somebody told me
how you had grown
as a man worthy
of honor on your own.

I wasn't there,
avoiding the weight
of giving you due care
forcing you to live enate

as I surrendered
to another life
that was false and rendered
me to live like one who died.

Now I come to you
to be absolved,
hoping to mask or subdue
a lifetime uninvolved.

First published in *Sixfold.*

Shaman on Wheels
(for John Gardner)

Waking to snow, thick as white paint
freshly applied to the ground but
smudged with tire tracks, boot prints
that took us to Batavia
as well as other places: Greece,
Sweden, Scandia, Vermont.

An American mythologist,
you could give the beast's perspective,
show us a laughing philosopher
debating Socrates, or
document a warrior
hunting to kill the Devil.

You were a wild man who proved
more moral than any priest, shaman,
elder, or cleric. Once, I grew
my hair long as drapery,
spilling over shoulders—as yours,
but mine was too generic

in contrast to your silvery
mane, locks reflected in the steel
side pipes of the motorcycle
you straddled on a mountain
in Pennsylvania, the one
that you rode into Asgard.

Mirrored Images
(for Jo Jo and Mom)

Two women sit, threading fingers,
intertwining generations.

Hands weave like vines of ivy
crawling along an ancient tree.

The mother—withered, infirm—
droops in the chair as she stares

at the other, her eyes vacant,
coated by the film of age.

The daughter—vibrant, lively—
rests soft palms over gnarled skin

that sags above bony fingers,
knuckles stiffened by arthritis.

So, the parent, now docile,
becomes nurtured by the child.

Shadows Over Sons

I did not live life defiled by hope
and went my own way for a decade.
Then, my mother, having been softened by age
and weary from too much drink, reached out.
We formed an uneasy alliance,
what might even be seen as a connection.

After time, my father and I gained ground,
solidified our lives still further when
we both outlived our wives. These days
what remains of my body seizes and groans
in unimagined pains, making strange sounds
as I imagine his cage of bones did as well at the end.

Dad died before I could hug him.
I'd hoped to ease and erase some memories—
the epiphanies of the strap or the bristles
of wire brushes, brutal punishments that made
military life a joy ride. I admit that
I waited too late. That weight's on us both.

First published in *Spectrum.*

Resurrection of Ponce

The push of volcanic eruptions
created this fabric of rocky land between
ocean and the Caribbean, its people now jarred
by shifting plates of earth, being battered
after so much damage, first Hugo,
then Maria, now Ian.

The stress of collapsed buildings rattled
the people, broken yet undefeated,
who will reach back to their indigenous
Taino roots. Ponce, cradle of native art,
will rise from rubble,
return to *Isla del Encanto*.

Greeting Marcielle

"I prefer Mars,"
she declares during sign-in
when asked for
her name of choice,

so she assumes
the port of the god of war.

The problem is—
if there is one—
she herself resists,
this militant pacifist,
this poet warrior.

First published in *SETU Western Voices.*

Three Acts on Oedipus Rex in Five Cinquains

Act 1
Left in
the desert by
his father after told
by oracles to kill his own
infant

Act 2
After
answering the
Sphynx's riddle, the young
Oedipus swears he will escape
that fate.

Hubris
overtakes him
as he commits the first
case of road rage on the journey
to Thebes.

Act 3
Zealous,
his search to learn
the truth reveals that he
killed the king who was also his
father.

Finale
He learns
from he who raised
him that none escape fate:
"Count no man as happy until
he dies."

First published in *Sixfold.*

Wunderkammer

Looking at the bric-a-brac
and debris of my life,
I rummage through events,
people, and experiences—
wondering how and where
I inventory
recollections.

Umberto Eco warned us
how terrifying
museums can be.
Do I sort and impose order,
or allow chaos? If order
is called for, what kind?

Where do I place the dreams
and nightmares that imposed themselves?
What of those prodigious
images, the clutter of life
and its collection of failures
or hopes, those
deferred disappointments?

Memories shine,
freshly painted
by fond recollection. Others
offer contrast but collapse
into rust as the erosion of time
destroys and smooths them
into something more palatable.

These cabinets of my mind
contain essentials, interests
that became the substance of me,
for like asters, life is created
out of a series of random acts—
buffeting winds that force me
to collide with time and people.

A Question of Longing

Gone already, forever?
Well, I wanted forever.

Souvenirs
in scrapbooks and drawers—
bare bones, evidence
of failure:
ticket stubs to *La Traviata*;
I wish it had been Wagner.
I could have been with you that much longer.
Others—one whole,
one torn—from the show
I saw alone.

There's a picture in my wallet.
A friend, a woman, told me
that being there
is "really making it".
I don't dare remove it.
I don't want to see it.
I do, actually, but
looking at your image
        smiling, hair
        falling over shoulders,
        holding the son
        I never had,
won't bring you any nearer, nor
put you any farther, and
it's as close
as I ever got

to you.

A Suadela's Shardoma

I feel the
edge of her nails as
her hand strokes
my arm. Her
inked dragonfly brings me to
the art of longing.

Enticing
me from the corner
of the bed,
one bare and
bended leg beckons, and I
lightly kiss her thigh.

First published in *Love Letters in Poetic Verse* (Southern Arizona Press, 2023).

It's Neither One Noir the Other

One unquiet night, sheets of grime,
rain-smeared, flow down graffiti-
painted bricks into potholes
and form puddles that reflect
multiple moons, to become fetid
footlights for a dingy stage.

The alley ends in an entrance
to a place reeking of spent cigars
and perfume so cheap it could be sold
by the bucket. Our moustachioed
black-market poet dapples his shadow
against the door's frosted glass pane.

He casts glances around the room,
makes sure the coast is clear, and giving
the look of a crooked dealer,
empties his pockets, spilling
random words into the open
palms of his customers, people

desiring to seize his offered *palabras*,
forming them into verses.
Their habit begins with innocence,
but then morphemes collide
and combine, becoming phrases,
a line here and there. Until somehow,

two are paired. Untwirling his cape,
he reveals lines, trapped behind stripes
of shadow and light. Soon enough,
couplets conjoin, divide; quatrains
morph into odes, then sonnets.
His users, now addicted, lose control.

A Chantey for Chantey
(a haibun-haiku)

Let's imbibe a chantey of the day I moved from child to seaman. Sailing Little Neck Bay with Billy Rose aboard *Chantey*, we raised sail, got underway. The old schooner was sound. We left the bay's safety as the noon-sun rose over the race—a place where confused waters of sound and ocean met and churned. Soon squall clouds grew over the bay while swelling white caps slapped *Chantey*. We tied loose gear and lashed canvas as harsh winds grew. At the foresail, I leaned into the bowsprit, pushing bare feet against the rope netting of the cat's cradle that hung over water. Working against time, I used the sheet's slack to tie a butterfly knot. The winds approached gale force, pushing *Chantey* hard over as water washed over gunwales, cascaded through the hatch, and flooded the cabin bay.

The main's gaff tore free, keeping us from lowering it. I climbed shaking ratlines to straddle the wooden spar and bring down the sail using my weight. While topside, I heard the squall shriek through cable shrouds and stays. Below, bow and sprit rose, dove, and danced in brutal swells. Turbulent currents drove *Chantey* diagonally, more leeward than forward, along an uncontrolled bearing toward the rocks of Hell's Gate. Gusts forced their way into the folds of the jib and undid my makeshift fastening to send the sail halfway up the forestay. Pelted red by a stinging rain, I retied the wayward sail, then made my way—hand over hand on lifelines—aft. Battened down, we rode the squall as best we could—wet, cold, and hanging on to whatever handhold we found. The storm passed as it rose—a momentary tempest—leaving us quiet in the bay.

Zimbabwean-born Matshona Dhliwayo once noted that "a sailor is not defined as much by how many seas he has sailed than by how many storms he has overcome." Bearing down a squall on the *Chantey* served as my graduation ceremony.

callous Neptune struck
with antagonistic winds
we weathered his worst

Blurring All Lines
(a Cento)

The night before you die, you wake at four
hearing the waves and the breathing shore,
the promise of the appalling air,
the compass needle dead on terror.

I stop at the border of dreams;
Norweigian Munch let out a silent scream.
An obstacle was often there,
but I guess I'm here. So I must take care.

There are lives in which nothing goes right:
a lonely impulse of delight,
the season of the lying equinox,
the heart that fed and the hand that mocked.

After the first astronauts reached heaven,
the voice was gravel, the gravel grain and then,
promised the permanence,
picture the resemblance.

With thanks to Louise Bogan, Jim Carroll, Constantine Cavafy, Stephen
Dobyns, William Everson (aka Brother Antonius), Carolyn Forche,
Lawrence Ferlinghetti, Galway Kinnell, Philip Levine, Robert Lowell,
Heather McHugh, W. S. Merwin, Reynolds Price, Carl Sandburg, Percy
Bysshe Shelley, William Butler Yeats, and especially my 9 Bridges cohorts.

And Then There's This

Coming out of Yonkers, Lawrence assumed
the throne of a proletarian prince
for the Beat generation.

He ended up in San Francisco by way of
Coney Island, a different breed who held court
in his citadel, City Lights.

His passion intensified the element
of surprise, inviting a state of being that rivals
the unself conscious.

Creating his own kind of koan,
he painted life by making the dragon a fly.
At 30, I met Ferlinghetti

as a man in his seventies;
I was pierced by the clarity
of his vision:

the sapphire eyes that saw into people
and bridged the gulf between them
to recalibrate the world.

About the Author

Bill Cushing lived in various states, the Virgin Islands, and Puerto Rico before moving to Glendale, California where he now resides with his wife and their son.

Returning to college after serving in the Navy and working on ships, classmates at the University of Central Florida called him the "blue collar poet" because of those earlier experiences. He then earned an MFA in creative non-fiction from Goddard College.

He is now semi-retired after nearly a quarter-century of teaching college English but continues to facilitate a writing group (9 Bridges) and collaborates with a local musician on a performance project they call "Notes and Letters."

Published in journals and anthologies, both online and in print, Bill is a multiple Pushcart Prize nominee, and his last chapbook , . . .*this just in.* . ., combines selected writings with visual art.

His first book *A Former Life* won a Kops-Fetherling International Book Award; his chapbook *Music Speaks* was honored at the 2019 San Gabriel Valley Poetry Festival and then with a 2021 New York City Book Award.

Bill is revising a memoir about his years working on ships but plans to return to his book *Counting Down the Breaths*, a work focused on his late wife's death to cancer written from the point of view of the caregiver.

Previous Titles

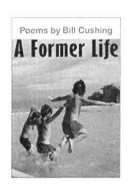

A Former Life

https://www.amazon.com/Former-Life-Bill-Cushing/dp/1635349389

Music Speaks

https://www.amazon.com/Music-Speaks-Bill-Cushing/dp/0359827012

… this just in …

https://www.amazon.com/this-just/dp/8182537460

Made in the USA
Las Vegas, NV
22 February 2023

67958794R00057